HILL-FORTS OF THE COTSWOLDS

Sean Campbell

AMBERLEY

Front cover: Crickley Hill from a distance.

First published 2016

Amberley Publishing
The Hill, Stroud
Gloucestershire, GL5 4EP

www.amberleybooks.com

Copyright © Sean Campbell, 2016

The right of Sean Campbell to be identified as the Author
of this work has been asserted in accordance with the
Copyrights, Designs and Patents Act 1988.

British Library Cataloguing in Publication Data.
A catalogue record for this book is available from the British Library.

ISBN 978 1 4456 6002 8 (print)
ISBN 978 1 4456 6003 5 (ebook)

Typesetting and Origination by Amberley Publishing.
Printed in Great Britain.

Contents

Acknowledgements

I would like to give many thanks to Jennifer and Primrose Campbell, and Heather and Gerard Campbell for their great support in aiding the expansion of this project. Thanks also to Timothy Darvill, John Gale, Paul Jefferies, Martin Williams and Charan Channe for their encouragement and guidance with this book. Also, a kind mention to the staff at Historic England Archives for their assistance with historical records.

This book is written from research gained between the period 2009–2016, using my photographs and interpretation on hill-forts and their defences, as well as highlighting other interpretations as well.

Overview: A Background to Hill-Forts

During the Late Bronze Age and Iron Age, in the period of *c.* 700–100 BC, there were enclosures built throughout Britain and Ireland – these enclosures are known as hill-forts (Darvill, 2011, 178). There are many potential reasons as to why these enclosures were built, and what the settlement or inner fort area would have been used for. Examples include protection for community settlement or stock, an area to farm (which could keep animals in and predators out), division between communities, a place to gather together/trade or symbolic gesture (to display power to other inhabitants of nearby areas). For this guide I will be concentrating on the defensive potential of hill-forts.

There are more than 3,300 hill-forts that have been recorded in Britain alone (Guilbert, 1981). The definition of a hill-fort has been a topic of debate for many years now, as not all hill-forts are positioned on a hill. However, other terms, such as 'defensive enclosure' or 'camp', cover too many defensive structures throughout history (Forde-Johnston, 1976; Hogg, 1975). There are also different spellings for these strongholds; the two main ones are hill-fort and hillfort. After assessing the sources used for this investigation, the spelling that will be used in this book is hill-fort.

The Main Types of Defences

The main defensive elements of a fort (fortification) are its ramparts, entrances and its positioning. There are three main types of defensive 'system': 'univallate', with one series of rampart (bank) and ditch surrounding the vulnerable areas; 'bi-vallate', with two separate banks and or ditches; and, 'multivallate', with more than two series of defences (Forde-Johnston, 1976).

There are three main types of rampart: (1) dump banks; (2) wooden palisades; and (3) ramparts built as walls, usually with either a stone facing or merely a timber frame filled with rubble or compacted earth core. Dump bank ramparts were built from the material dug from a ditch, which was then piled up to form a bank; and this material would have settled at an angle of rest (Harding, 1976).

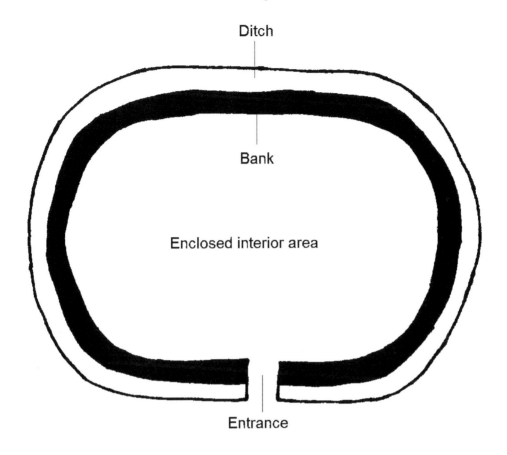

The layout of a hill-fort.

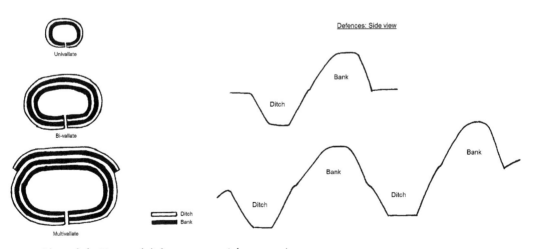

Above left: Types of defences, an aerial perspective.

Above right: Side view of defences.

Simple bank and ditch defence

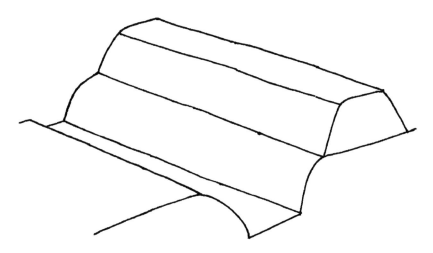

Simple bank and ditch defence.

The use of wooden palisades (strong fencing) is probably the next simplest form of defence; timber would have been a strong material to use for this, but it was not always available. The posts are normally found to have been spaced out, probably to save on timber. It can be assumed that this defence would have been primarily to keep out animals or thieves, as it gives the defenders no real advantage in height against any attackers determined to break through (Hogg, 1975).

Wooden palisade fencing

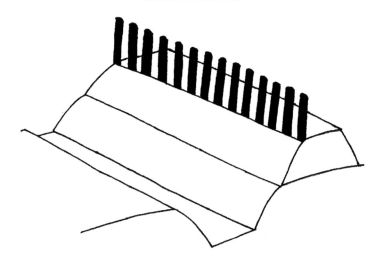

Wooden palisade defence.

Revetment in the form of walls were also used at sites to give additional strength to the ramparts. Walls are the most complex of defensive structures built at forts. Their aim was to present a front that was vertical or near vertical to anyone approaching the site. The stone face was also useful as not only was it prevented from fire attack but, even if it was knocked down, it still would have been a difficult task to get through the heavy broken stone (Harding, 1976).

The combination of the ditch working with the bank would have made breaching the fort a difficult task, as there was more than one element to the defences. At some sites there was also a 'berm', a level section of ground between the bank and ditch defences.

Wall defence.

Multivallate defences at Kimsbury Castle.

Entrances

The weakest part of any hill-fort would have been its entrance and so, as a result, few forts have more than two (Dyer, 1990). The entrances were not fixed solidly, and the gateways, usually timber, would have been vulnerable to being battered down or burnt down with fire (Hogg, 1975). Other ways of protecting the entrance at some sites were through complex positioning and hidden hollow-ways (RCHME, 1975). Many of the early gates were simple straight access but, as time went on, more works were being built at either end of long barbican passages, almost hidden in claw-like outworks. As well as entrances that were set obliquely between staggered ramparts. Also, at some sites, the entrances may not have even been present. The fact that some entrances had been blocked by felled tree trunks shows the severe fear that some had of the opposition (Dyer, 1990).

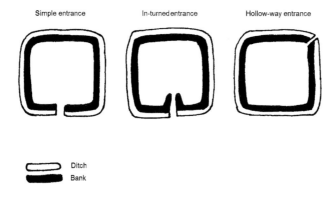

Examples of different entrances.

One of the entrances at Uley Bury.

It is clear from the evidence found at sites, mainly through excavation, that other devices associated with the entrances were used to give more defence to the fort. These consist mainly of guard chambers and outworks. These guard chambers were set into the ends of the ramparts behind the entrance gates (Megaw and Simpson, 1979).

Positioning

The main types of locations on which you will find hill-forts positioned can vary from a hill-top situation, with all sides of the fort sloping downwards, to a low-lying position, where the surrounding ground is relatively flat. Some examples of positions are hill-top, promontory, cliff and plateau-edged, hill-sloped and low-lying (Forde-Johnston, 1976). There are also many different shapes in which forts were built; some follow the natural edges of the land and others do not.

Whether a hill-fort is positioned on high or low ground, with the advantage of natural sloping ground or not, there are many reasons for these positions being chosen. These include being close to existing settlements, near to supplies (such as water, food, building materials), suitable for the resources, the best location in the vicinity or a dominant position, as well as perhaps being a suitable position for the community that built the fort (Hill and Jesson, 1971).

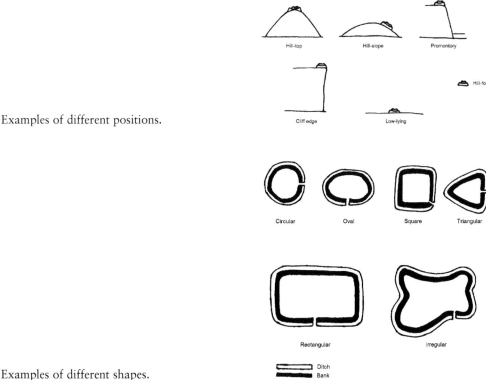

Examples of different positions.

Examples of different shapes.

The high dominant positioning of Uley Bury.

The Historic Cotswolds

The Cotswolds is an Area of Outstanding Natural Beauty (AONB), encompassing parts of six counties: Gloucestershire, Oxfordshire, Somerset, Warwickshire, Wiltshire and Worcestershire (Macleod, 2011). The highest point reaches 310 metres above sea level at Cleeve Cloud, Southam (Darvill, 2011). The Cotswolds is distinguished by its creamy white oolite limestone, which formed underneath the surface (Copeland, 2013).

A great view from Cleeve Common.

A view of Cleeve Common in the distance, from near Hewletts Camp.

The Cotswolds: Area of Outstanding Natural Beauty.

There is a vast variety of archaeological monuments that were built in this area, many of which are still visible today, including long barrows, causewayed enclosures and many more examples. Of the counties that the Cotswolds covers, Gloucestershire takes up most of the area. It is described by Professor Timothy Darvill in his book *Prehistoric Gloucestershire*: 'The quality and quantity of upstanding prehistoric monuments in and around Gloucestershire is quite exceptional' (Darvill, 2011, 17).

I have really enjoyed spending time in the beautiful countryside of the Cotswolds, where there are many areas to discover and plenty of outstanding views to be seen. There are numerous paths to explore in this area, many of which are located along the Cotswold Way. This route measures 102 miles long and was launched by Gloucestershire County Council in 1970 (Copeland, 2013).

A Cotswold Way signpost at Leckhampton Hill.

The Hill-Forts of the Cotswolds

Within the Cotswolds, I have recorded forty-five hill-forts (which include some sites that are probable or possible forts). There are three sites for which I could not find formal names on records, so I have called them Dowdeswell Hill, Idbury Hill and Owlpen. The sites recorded as possible or probable hill-forts are Birdlip Camp, Dowdeswell Hill, Hawkesbury Knoll, Icomb Camp, Owlpen, Roel Camp and Stow Camp. I have drawn a map of the Cotswolds boundary, based on the map from a Google Maps application. Within the Cotswolds, there is a wide range of different defences built, of varying shapes, sizes and positions.

The positions of the hill-forts of the Cotswolds in relation to each other.

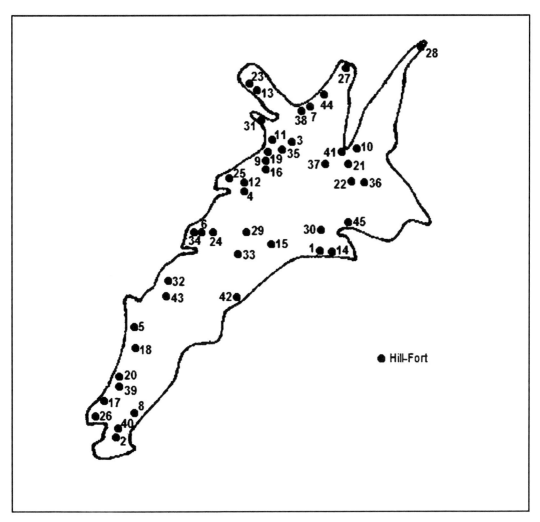

An annotated map of the positioning of these forts: 1. Ablington Camp, 2. Bathampton Camp, 3. Beckbury Camp, 4. Birdlip Camp, 5. Brackenbury Ditches, 6. The Bulwarks, 7. Burhill, 8. Bury Wood Camp, 9. The Castles, Dowdeswell, 10. Chastleton Barrow, 11. Cleeve Cloud, 12. Crickley Hill, 13. Danes Camp, 14. Dean Camp, 15. Ditches Hillfort, 16. Dowdeswell Hill, 17. Dyrham Camp, 18. Hawkesbury Knoll, 19. Hewletts Camp, 20. Horton Camp, 21. Icomb Camp, 22. Idbury Hill, 23. Kemerton Camp, 24. Kimsbury Castle, 25. Leckhampton Hill, 26. Little Down, 27. Meon Hill, 28. Nadbury Camp, 29. Norbury Camp, Colesbourne 30. Norbury Camp, Northleach and Eastington 31. Nottingham Hill, 32. Owlpen, 33. Pinbury Hillfort, 34. Ring Hill, 35. Roel Camp, 36. The Roundabout, 37. Salmonsbury Camp, 38. Shenberrow Hillfort, 39. Sodbury Camp, 40. Solsbury Hill, 41. Stow Camp, 42. Trewsbury Fort, 43. Uley Bury, 44. Willersey Hill Camp, 45. Windrush Camp.

The main sources I have used are the Royal Commission on Historic Monuments (England) and their work on the Gloucestershire Cotswolds, online monument records and referenced text from other book sources. The dimensions that have been given in this book are accurate to when they were originally measured.

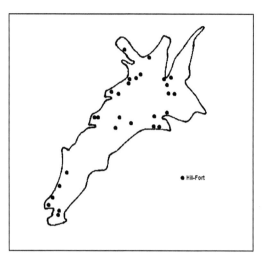 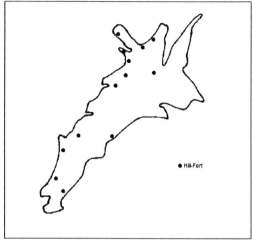

Above left: Univallate-defended forts' positioning.

Above right: Bi-vallate-defended forts' positioning.

Multivallate-defended forts' positioning.

Each hill-fort has been discussed in alphabetical order and listed with the name and location, with photographs taken where possible to show their features that are still visible in the landscape today.

Ablington Camp (Bibury)

A univallate fort positioned at the edge of a plateau (SP 105074) above the River Coln at 400 feet O.D. The ground at the edge of the plateau was steep, and would have offered protection to the north side. The location of the river being so close would have been a useful resource for those inhabiting this site at the time. The bank defences to the south and west are about 27 feet wide and not more than 1 foot high; to the east, the defence is up to 5 feet high (RCHME, 1976, 13–14).

The interior area enclosed is 8 acres, with three possible entrances. The main entrance occurs where there is a gap in the bank to the south-east. A second entrance is in the north-east corner, where there is a narrow gap. There is also a hollow-way leading up from the river at the end of the bank to the north-west (RCHME, 1976, 13-14).

Ablington Camp: a view of the River Coln, a potential water source.

Bathampton Camp (Bathampton)

A large univallate hill-fort covering some 80 acres (ST 7745 6502). Now positioned on this fort is a modern golf course. The rampart is made out of stone and some field boundaries appear to overlie the ditch defence (OS Map 1961 and Wainright, 1967, cited in Pastscape, 2004). The wall has been measured to have been 9.5 feet wide, with a 12 feet berm in between the wall and a flat-bottomed ditch (Cunliffe, 1974, 235). Walking along the footpath that runs through the golf course, I was able to identify some ground features that perhaps were original earthworks of this fort.

Beckbury Camp (Temple Guiting)

When I was walking in the fields along the path on relatively flat ground, I could see a long rampart defence in the distance – it looked impressive on approach. It is positioned on the edge of a plateau (SP 064299) and encloses an interior area of 5.5 acres. This site had univallate defences; the bank is 25 feet wide and 5 feet above the interior level. It was built along the east and south sides, and there is evidence of an outer ditch that has mostly been levelled. Fire-reddened stones were used as part of the outside face of the bank and were found on the east side. The north and west sides had no ramparts, but there was the plateau edge for protection (RCHME, 1976, 116–117). The large bank defence is still visible and stands tall today.

Beckbury Camp: the bank defences stand out on approach.

Beckbury Camp: the steep bank seen from the exterior.

Beckbury Camp: the good views over lower ground seen on approach to this site.

Beckbury Camp: a view of the fort from a distance.

The entrance was probably situated at the end of the bank at the south-west corner, where there is a 40-foot-wide gap (RCHME, 1976, 116–117). There is a hollow-way on the north-west side that leads down to some springs. There have been flint arrowheads and Iron Age pottery found at this site (Copeland, 2013, 37).

Birdlip Camp (Cowley)

At this site is an alleged hill-fort, positioned on a promontory (SO 925150) (RCHME, 1976, 39). This site, which is also known as Peak Camp, overlooks the Severn Vale (Darvill, 2011, 64). It is positioned close to Crickley hill-fort at Coberley, which can be seen in the distance on approach to this site. On visiting this area, the original earthworks were not clearly identifiable, but the natural advantage of the steep edges of the promontory was evident and showed that from this side it would not have been approachable.

The area enclosed has been recorded as about 2.5 acres and is now occupied by woodland. The fort defences were bi-vallate, but the two curving and concentric banks have been reduced by quarrying and ploughing. Excavations took place in 1980/81 and the outer bank was recorded to have survived to a height of only 1 foot tall, while the outer ditch had been re-cut four times (Copeland, 2013, 75–76).

Birdlip Camp: the area is now covered with trees.

Brackenbury Ditches (North Nibley)

This hill-fort is positioned on a spur of the Cotswold escarpment (ST 747949) and it encloses an area of 4 acres. Along with the high positioning, rampart defences were built along the top of the sloping sides. To give extra protection there are two series of ramparts along the plateau side. The fort defences were partly bi-vallate, and to the north-east there was an outer rampart, 25 feet wide and 5 feet tall. It had an external ditch, which is 20 feet wide and 4 feet deep (RCHME, 1976, 86–87).

The inner defences surrounded the tip of the spur. On the north-east side there is a 50-foot-wide and a 10-foot-high rampart, with a 45-foot-wide and 8-foot-deep external ditch. This ditch is separated from the rampart by an 8-foot-wide berm. The rampart reduces in size on the north-west and south-east sides, 20 feet above the ditch and with a counterscarp bank drops down to follow a ledge from the north corner. The entrance to the interior area was 10 feet wide on the south-east side and would have been accessed from the plateau through an entrance gap 20 feet wide in the outer defence. From the vale the fort was accessed via a hollow-way (RCHME, 1976, 86–87).

The spectacular views, which can be seen from the summit, emphasise the high ground positioning upon which this fort was built.

Brackenbury Ditches: the steep approach to the summit.

Brackenbury Ditches: the positional advantage over lower areas.

Brackenbury Ditches: some earthwork remains at this fort.

Brackenbury Ditches: some earthwork remains near to the interior area.

Brackenbury Ditches: the interior area.

Brackenbury Ditches: this site gives great views over nearby areas.

The Bulwarks (Haresfield)

This univallate fort (SO 829091), built 630 yards east of Ring Hill, is irregular in shape and covers a large area. The defences, which can be seen from the road, consist of a single bank and outer ditch. The bank, 45 feet wide and 7 feet high, is of a glacis construction externally and has a wide ledge running along the inner side that is 2 feet high and up to 10 feet wide. The outer ditch was 40 feet wide and 7 feet deep. The other sides were defended by the natural edge, and by the positioning of Ring Hill to the west (RCHME, 1976, 62–64). This bank defence, which is long and high and thus stands out from a distance, can be seen from the road.

There are four gaps in the bank, along with corresponding causeways in the ditch, which perhaps were original entrances. There was also a hollow-way that entered the ditch at the north end via a gully (RCHME, 1976, 62–64). The close positioning of this fort in relation to Ring Hill indicates that perhaps there was a relationship between these two enclosures. It has been considered that perhaps this fort formed an annexe to Ring Hill (Copeland, 2013, 94).

The Bulwarks: a view from a distance, from next to the road.

The Bulwarks: this large bank, from the side.

The Bulwarks: the bank defence.

Burhill (Buckland)

This is a univallate defended fort, positioned on a spur of the Cotswold escarpment (SP 085363). There are a bank and ditch, the parts of the bank that have survived measuring 25 feet wide and 5 feet tall, the outer ditch being 30 feet wide and 3 feet deep (RCHME, 1976, 22–23).

Burhill: the fort remains on approach.

Burhill: the bank seen from the exterior.

The positioning of this fort perhaps was not the most advantageous, as there is higher ground nearby that overlooks this enclosure, although the fort itself does overlook many areas in the distance.

Burhill: a view of the defence from the interior.

Burhill: looking along the bank defence.

There are some remains of the defensive earthworks still visible today; on approach to this fort, I could see the rampart stand out in the distance from a nearby field.

Burhill: the inside of this fort at sunset.

Burhill: good views over nearby areas can be seen from this location.

Bury Wood Camp (Colerne)

Bury Wood Camp: the end of the outer bank defence.

A bi-vallate-defended fortification, also known as Bury Ditches, is sub-triangular in plan and is positioned on a promontory (Centred ST 818740). Where there are no natural defences, there are bank and ditch defences on the south-west. There is also evidence of enclosures being built within the fort, identified on aerial photographs (OS map 1955 and Mellor, 1935–7, 504, cited in Pastscape, 1999). I reached this area via a footpath and, even though the site itself was not accessible, the edge of the outer rampart could be seen from the track below.

The Castles (Dowdeswell)

This fort is positioned on a spur (SO 999191); it is near rectangular in shape and has univallate defences. It is situated on slightly sloping ground at 700 feet O. D. (RCHME, 1976 43–44). The rampart defences have been damaged at parts of this site, but some of the earthworks are still clearly visible.

The Castles, Dowdeswell: the defences on approach.

The Castles, Dowdeswell: the rampart defence, from the outside.

To the south-west where the rampart is best preserved, 23 feet across, 4 feet above the interior level and 8 feet above the ditch fill. The ditch measured 25 feet across; it has been disturbed by a track and has been filled largely to the north-west side, where there is a suggestion of a slight counterscarp bank. A terrace extending downwards is 20 feet below the scarp, which marks the edge of the enclosed area. The interior area is 14.5 acres, and the original entrance appears to be positioned at the south-east corner (RCHME, 1976, 43-44).

The Castles, Dowdeswell: the rampart remains.

The Castles, Dowdeswell: the interior, seen from the outside.

The path along the track enables you to walk alongside the rampart. I was impressed with this site, as walking along the main track I could see the south rampart, which stood out on approach.

The Castles, Dowdeswell: the defences can be clearly seen along the path.

The Castles, Dowdeswell: the fort from a distance.

Chastleton Barrow (Chastleton)

This univallate fort, positioned on almost level ground (SP 259283), is circular in plan and encloses an area of 3.5 acres; it is also known as Chastleton Camp. The rampart defences were faced with large stone blocks and probably also with a rubble core (Dyer, 1970, 50).

Chastleton Barrow: the circular defences seen from the interior.

Chastleton Barrow: a view of the enclosed interior.

Excavation has shown the defensive wall to be 20 feet wide at the base and 12 feet high in places. There is no sign of a ditch. There are two entrances to this fort, one at the east and another at the north-west (Dyer, 1970, 50).

Chastleton Barrow: the entrance.

Chastleton Barrow: the rampart is now covered with trees.

Chastleton Barrow: a view from a nearby road.

On visiting this site, I could see the bank, which is now marked by trees, stand out in the distance. It does seem that the positioning is not defensively strong as, on approach, it does not hold high ground advantage. However, the built defences do cover all areas of this enclosure.

Cleeve Cloud (Southam)

This semi-circular hill-fort was built near a cliff edge (SO 985255) and covers an area of about 3 acres of sloping ground (RCHME, 1976, 106–108). This site is an intriguing site as its positioning means that it can be overlooked by nearby areas of Cleeve Common, which now has a golf course. It does have the cliff-edge advantage for protection, and perhaps this was more important than being overlooked.

The defences built were bi-vallate, with each bank and ditch about 30 feet across. The banks are between 8.5 feet to 11 feet high above the ditches. There is an intermediate berm, which separated the inner ditch from the outer bank; it is 30 feet wide in some areas, but only half the width of this in other parts. There is no surviving entrance at this site (RCHME, 1976, 106–108).

The Cleeve Common ground on which this fort was built is the highest area in the Cotswolds at 310 metres above sea level (Darvill, 2011, 31) and offers great views over the lower ground. The enclosed area is comparatively small in relation to the area that the defences cover, some of the remains are still surviving today.

Cleeve Cloud: the bank defences seen from the interior.

Cleeve Cloud: the fort on approach.

Cleeve Cloud: the outer bank defence.

Cleeve Cloud: the inside area of this fort.

Cleeve Cloud: distant areas can be seen for miles.

Cleeve Cloud: the fort was built up to this steep edge.

Crickley Hill (Coberley)

A fantastic example of an Early Iron Age hill-fort is located in Coberley, built on a promontory position (SO 927161), with steep sides surrounding most sides of the interior area. The side that is not defended by the natural edges has a univallate defence (RCHME, 1976, 33–34). This area was previously occupied in the Neolithic period; a Causewayed enclosure was discovered (Darvill, 2011, 64). When visiting this site, I was impressed at the condition of the earthwork remains, where the rampart is clearly visible. The interior area enclosed is 9.5 acres, and the fort is triangular in shape. There was one entrance at this site, which was its weakest point of defence. Even though most of the site was protected by the steep sides, the approach to the entrance site was relatively flat when compared to the nearby land outside the enclosure. Therefore, this entrance and the rampart came under heavy attack (RCHME, 1976, 33–34).

The defences consist of a single bank and ditch, with traces of a ditch further beyond. Excavation has shown that there were three phases in which these defences were built and then rebuilt as the result of attacks, which included fire. Phase one consisted of post holes along the rampart. Phase two had a timber-laced rampart with facing walls about 23 feet apart. A berm 2 feet to 5 feet wide was in between the rampart and flat-bottomed ditch; the ditch was about 24 feet across and 6 feet deep. There was an entrance that had front and rear gates, and buildings were built on either side outside of the fort. In phase three, the defences

Crickley Hill: the rampart defence on approach.

Crickley Hill: the rampart remains from the interior.

Crickley Hill: the entrance.

Crickley Hill: a view of the entrance from the outside.

Crickley Hill: great views seen from within this fort.

Crickley Hill: the rampart and ditch defence from the exterior.

had to be rebuilt as they were burnt down previously; these consisted of solid bastions with irregular curved walls that flanked the gate. This was protected by an out-turned horn work with curved walls and a ditch, which was partly built over the pre-existing ditch. This existing ditch was modified further to enhance the defences; however, these defences were also burnt down (RCHME, 1976, 33–34).

This fort's high positioning would also have meant that it would have been visible from afar and probably would have been a dominating feature in the landscape. The views of the surrounding areas are very good and, looking north from the fort edge, you can see a long way in the distance.

Danes Camp (Conderton)

This univallate fort, which is also known as Conderton Camp, is positioned on the south side of Bredon Hill (SO 972384), nearby to Kemerton Camp. It is the smaller of the two forts on Bredon Hill, enclosing an area of about 3 acres. This site, near oval in shape, utilises the steep sloping sides on all faces except the north. Excavations in 1958/59 showed that the site was originally a corral for livestock. The single bank and outer ditch defence was built around the interior area, and in places there was a counter scarp bank. There are two entrances at this fort – one in the centre of the north side, and another at the south end (Darvill, Stamper and Timby 2002, 201).

Danes Camp: the steep sloping sides, from the path.

Danes Camp: looking up a steep side.

Danes Camp: the pathway, with the fort in the distance.

The site was modified in the first century BC in the form of a bank dividing off the north end. No ditch was associated with it, and round houses were built within this area (Darvill, Stamper and Timby, 2002, 201). From the footpath that runs parallel to this fort, I could see that the steep sides to this fort would have given the inhabitants an advantage over anyone approaching from these sides. There is a level approach to one of the sides, where there is an entrance.

Dean Camp (Coln. St Aldwyns)

Positioned on a spur of Great Oolite (SP 165087) is a univallate hill-fort, which encloses an area of 12 acres. The entrance was probably to the east where there is a gap in the bank. The bank defences, 40 feet wide and 6 feet high, are positioned on the east and north-east sides, with no ditch visible. The north and west sides had a short scarp, which does not continue at the south section. There are nearby water sources: the river Leach and a tributary (RCHME, 1976, 36–37). On visiting the area, even though I was unable to access the site of the fort, I was able to see that the ground it was positioned on was not particularly high in relation to nearby areas.

Ditches Hillfort (North Cerney)

A univallate defended fort (SO 996095) with an enclosed interior area covering about 10 acres. The north half of the site has a curving boundary; the south half drops down to a slight spur on the Great Oolite ridge. The ditch remains that were visible on the north and west sides are about 40 feet wide and up to 3 feet deep below a bank. It is indicated that the bank on the west side was of spread stone (RCHME, 1976, 85–86). When visiting near this site, the fort remains were not clearly visible from a distance on ground level from a nearby road.

Excavations took place at this site during 1982/83 and showed that the fort first had a stone rampart or wall, with an unusual irregular rock-cut inner ditch during the first century BC. In the early first century AD, a second ditch was added, which was dug on the outer side of the bank. The main entrance, located to the north-east, was gated but it was not heavily defended. At the south-west were paired ditches extending outwards and forming a funnel-shaped entrance approach. Geophysical survey revealed that there was a large round house, situated more or less in the centre of the fort (Darvill, 2011, 226–228). The fort remains were not clearly visible from a distance on ground level from a nearby road.

Dowdeswell Hill (Dowdeswell)

A possible hill-fort positioned on sloping ground (SP 005186), it was identified on aerial photographs. The defensive ditch, 3 feet wide across the bottom and 5 feet deep in a section that had been exposed by quarrying. Another section of ditch was exposed by a pipe trench, the V-shaped ditch, 5 feet wide and 2.5 feet deep. On the west side there is an annex to the enclosure. This site has been heavily damaged by quarrying (Gloucester City Mus., 1958, and RCHM, 1971, cited in Pastscape, 2009). On visiting this site situated next to Kilkenny viewpoint, I was not able to clearly identify any of the original fort remains, although I was able to see that there are views over distant areas for miles.

Dyrham Camp (Dyrham and Hinton)

This fort, also known as Hinton Hill, enclosed an area of about 12 acres and is positioned on a spur of the Cotswold escarpment (ST 741767). The defences used are univallate, with the rampart 35 feet wide, 8 feet high above the interior, and about 13 feet above the 20-foot-wide outer ditch (RCHME, 1976, 51). This site, near triangular in shape, follows the scarp edges, which would have given natural defence to the site (Copeland, 2013, 140–141).

The entrance is positioned in the centre of the defences on the east side, where a modern road now goes through it (RCHME, 1976, 51). Walking through the fields along the path to the south of this fort, you can see it in the distance. Some of the defences are still visible from the road.

Dyrham Camp: a view of this fort from a distance.

Dyrham Camp: the fort at the top, in the distance.

Dyrham Camp: the defences, seen on approach.

Dyrham Camp: the rampart defence, seen from nearby the road.

Hawkesbury Knoll (Hawkesbury)

Hawkesbury Knoll: the steep sides surrounding the summit.

It is recorded that a possible univallate hill-fort once existed on Hawkesbury Knoll (ST 768872); however, there are no earthworks of Iron Age type discovered (RCHME, 1976, 64). There is a long barrow monument situated at the summit of this hill (Copeland, 2013, 132), and perhaps the positioning of this fort was linked to this. On visiting this location, I can see why this would have been a suitable place to build a fort, as the high ground, surrounded by sloping edges, would have offered a good position from which to defend.

Hewletts Camp (Cheltenham)

An irregularly shaped univallate fort (SO 98142244), measuring about 100 yards long and 60 yards wide. The sides of the hill have been scarped to form a steep slope. On the west side, there is a bank and ditch about 35 yards long (Witts, 1874–80, 204, cited in

Pastscape, 1968). Due to its location, I was not able to reach the site itself. I was able to see that the positioning would have given some height advantage over nearby areas, but is approachable without much exertion.

Horton Camp (Horton)

This univallate hill-fort, also known as 'The Castles', is situated on a spur of the Cotswold escarpment (ST 764844); the defensive rampart is clearly visible and its size is impressive. The rampart was 40 feet wide and 10 feet high, and the outer ditch was 25 feet wide, although it has been mostly filled in and is traceable by the soil changes. There is a slight bank along the scarp edge near the south-east corner, which stretches 100 feet to the west (RCHME, 1976, 65–66).

The approach to this fort from the west side is a steep climb; this site's positioning made use of the natural defence of the steep edges. On the north-east side where the rampart was built, the approach is level, but the defences built are of high stature.

The original entrance was probably at the south-east corner, with a second entrance perhaps represented by a hollow-way and located 300 feet to the west of the original entrance – it has been partly damaged by strip lynchets. The shape of this fort is irregular and encloses an area of just under 5 acres (RCHME, 1976, 65–66).

Horton Camp: next to the large rampart, taken within the interior.

Horton Camp: the rampart seen from outside the fort.

Horton Camp: the rampart defence.

Horton Camp: the steep approach to this fort from the naturally defended sides.

Horton Camp: the interior area.

Horton Camp: some areas have been worn down, but it is generally well preserved.

Icomb Camp (Icomb)

A probable hill-fort, which has now been mostly destroyed, stands on Icomb Hill (SP 205230). The bank, which survived, is 30 feet wide and generally under 1 foot high. Meanwhile, a ditch formerly on the north side can be traced for about 780 yards. There is evidence to suggest there were discontinuous ditches on the south slope, which perhaps indicates that this relatively large site was unfinished (RCHME, 1976, 66–67). When I visited this site's location I was unable to firmly locate any evidence of the defence remains from ground level.

Idbury Hill (Idbury)

A univallate fort, near oval in plan, is situated on the west side of Westcote Hill (SP 2288 1955) and encloses an area of about 8.6 acres. The rampart, which is aligned north-east to south-west, survives at about 33 feet wide and a little over 1 foot high. Originally the rampart was revetted with a limestone dry walling and would have stood much higher. Beyond the rampart is a large quarry ditch, about 49 feet wide and identifiable as a darker band of soil. The entrance is situated on the north side (EH scheduling revision, 1996, cited in Pastscape, 2009). I was not able to identify any fort remains from the side of the road. However, in the field, I could see slight colour changes in the ground markings, which perhaps mark the original fort defences.

Kemerton Camp (Kemerton)

This fort, positioned on a spur on the north side of the hill (SO 958402), is also known as Bredon Hill, and is situated 2 kilometres from Conderton Camp. The strong positioning of this fort takes advantage of the natural sloping sides to the north-west and north-east. The defences used at this site are bi-vallate and these protect the other sides. Excavations have shown that the first line of defence built at this fort, perhaps of sixth-century origin BC, is the outer rampart of the current earthworks. The bank is about 44 feet wide at the base and over 9.5 feet high, with a dry-stone walling on the outer face, and a sloping rear face. A berm separated this rampart and a V-shaped ditch that was about 33 feet wide and 15 feet deep. The enclosed area of about 17.5 acres had no known entrances (Darvill, Stamper & Timby, 2002, 194).

At a later date, perhaps the second century BC, the inner rampart was added and is of glacis construction. There is no berm but a continuous slope of about 36 feet from the bottom of the ditch to the top of the rampart, where a timber breastwork was probably built along the top. There is a single entrance near the centre of the defences that was modified several times, and is now identifiable as the ends of in-turned ramparts creating a narrow entrance, which originally was walled and gated. As well as two other entrances built into the outer rampart, the inner rampart was constructed, and they are positioned near the cliff edge at either end. The area of the second phase is half of the area enclosed during the first phase (Darvill, Stamper and Timby, 2002, 194).

Kemerton Camp: a view from the inner rampart.

Kemerton Camp: next to the steep inner rampart defence.

Kemerton Camp: looking through the inner entrance.

Kemerton Camp: the in-turned entrance.

Kemerton Camp: the ditch and rampart defences.

Kemerton Camp: the deep inner-ditch defence.

The earthwork remains of the bank and ditch defences are clearly visible and, on approach, I could see the defences stand out in the distance. This is an impressive site, with lots of remains to see.

Kimsbury Castle (Painswick)

This impressive fort, which has multivallate defences, is positioned on a spur of the Cotswold escarpment (SO 869121). This enclosure is also known as Painswick Beacon or Castle Godwyn. There are three ramparts and two medial ditches protecting this site. Overall these defences are up to 180 feet wide on the west, south-east and north-east sides. The inner rampart is of glacis construction and measures 5 feet above the interior; it continues on the north along the edge of a short steep scarp as a bank without a ditch. The middle rampart rises from the edge of the inner ditch and is separated from its outer ditch by a 15-feet-wide berm. The outer rampart turns west at the north-east corner for 350 feet following a sloping terrace (RCHME, 1976, 91–93).

This fort encloses an area of 7 acres; this interior area has been damaged by quarrying and there is part of a golf course situated on this site. There appears to have been two entrances to the interior. At the main entrance near the south-east corner the banks either side of the entrance do not line up, while on the east side the bank is in-turned and curves around to the west for 80 feet. The west-side inner bank turns in also straight towards the interior for 60 feet (RCHME, 1976, 91–93). This elongated entrance would

Kimsbury Castle: a dominant feature in the landscape.

Kimsbury Castle: looking down from the inner rampart.

have given greater control over who entered the fort (Darvill, 2011, 190). A second entrance may have existed at the north-west corner where a hollow-way is flanked by the inturning of the inner bank, leading to the interior area (RCHME, 1976, 91–93).

Kimsbury Castle: the rampart-and-ditch combination.

Kimsbury Castle: great views from the top of the inner rampart.

This hill-fort would have relied greatly on its visual impact that it has in the landscape (Darvill, 2011, 190). Its striking earthworks would have been a dominating feature, displaying its defences to any potential threats looking on. This site is a fantastic example of a hill-fort, as it has strong and strategically built defences that not only would have been a challenging task to breach themselves, but that also had the additional advantage of the high ground positioning.

Kimsbury Castle: a view of distant areas.

Kimsbury Castle: the rampart defences stand out on approach.

Leckhampton Hill (Leckhampton)

Positioned on a spur of the Cotswold escarpment (SO 948183), this hill-fort encloses an area of about 7 acres. There are univallate defences built on the east and south sides. The north and west sides are protected by the quarried scarp edges (RCHME, 1976, 77–78).

Leckhampton Hill: a view of the rampart defence on approach.

Leckhampton Hill: the defences, seen from the entrance.

Excavations in 1925 and 1969 revealed that the rampart had been burnt south of the entrance. The rampart was originally about 20 feet wide and up to 6 feet tall, and was made of a stone core revetment, with dry-stone walls tied at the bottom with transverse timbers. The outer wall was 3 feet thick and 1 feet and 8 inches tall; the inner wall had not been well preserved. The outer ditch was up to 14 feet wide and 9 feet deep; the bank and ditch are separated by a 3-foot-wide berm. There is another earthwork about 350 yards east of the fort, which perhaps was connected (RCHME, 1976, 77–78).

Leckhampton Hill: the rampart remains, seen from within this fort.

Leckhampton Hill: the defences from the outside.

The entrance is positioned in the bank to the east. Semi-circular guard chambers were positioned either side of the entrance and were inset into the ramparts (RCHME, 1976, 77–78). This high ground location gives it a dominating position over the lower ground. On approach to this site, along the pathway, I could see the remains of the south rampart; it stood out in the distance and, like most of the rest of this site, it is still visible to see today.

Leckhampton Hill: looking through the entrance into the interior.

Leckhampton Hill: the impressive views seen from this fort.

Little Down (North Stoke)

This univallate hill-fort, positioned on a promontory (ST 709 689), is triangular in plan. The entrance is in the middle of the eastern side (Copeland, 2013, 149).

Little Down: the defences can be seen on the approach.

Little Down: the rampart defence from the outside.

There is an irregularity in the bank, while the ditch shows different depths across the fort; these are indications that perhaps this fort was unfinished. There was perhaps an outer rampart south of the entrance where there is a ground feature, although this could be a round barrow (Copeland, 2013, 149).

Little Down: the ditch defence.

Little Down: the interior

Positioned on high ground, I could see the high-ground advantage this fort has. The fort was accessible along level ground, but the rampart defences were built strongly along this side and are still visible today.

Little Down: the rampart, from the interior.

Little Down: the entrance.

Meon Hill (Quinton)

Meon Hill: the fort, situated at the summit in the distance.

This multivallate fort is positioned on a hill-top (SP 176453). There are two banks, three ditches and a counterscarp bank, which follows the contours of the enclosure. On the west-north-west side there is a single bank where the hill falls steeply. There is evidence of a dry-stone wall to the north side of the middle bank, which might be an original feature. There has been ploughing to the earthworks mainly on the north side (OS Survey 1955 and Thomas, 1960, 205 cited in Pastscape, 2004).

From a nearby footpath I was able to see that the positioning of this fort is in a strong position; however, I was unable to clearly identify any earthworks close up, as the fort itself was inaccessible.

Nadbury Camp (Ratley and Upton)

This probably multivallate fort (centred on SP 39025 48203) has been visible on aerial photographs; however, this site has been heavily levelled as a result of ploughing. The fort appears to be defined by an inner and outer bank, with a ditch in-between. At the west corner there appears to be an entrance, where an out-turned ditch ends. There is a series of parallel crescent-shaped banks and an additional ditch on the eastern side, which perhaps was an annexe or complex entranceway (NMR Aerial Photograph 1947 and Next Perspectives PGA 2007, cited in Pastscape, 2013).

I accessed the area next to this fort via a footpath next to the main road. The fort itself was inaccessible; however, from the path I could see a raised line of ground, which perhaps is remains of the bank defences.

Norbury Camp (Colesbourne)

This univallate fort is positioned on a hill-top (SO 990150) and probably enclosed an area of about 8 acres. To the south there is a bank 18 feet wide and 3 feet high, with an outer ditch 20 feet wide and 3 feet deep. To the east there is a scarp 2.5 feet high, and at the north-east there is a slight scarp to the ditch. There is an entrance at the south-west end, where the bank ends overlap (RCHME, 1976, 34–35). I was only able to see this site from a distance, but the positioning did seem a suitable site from which to defend.

Norbury Camp (Northleach and Eastington)

A large univallate fort covering 80 acres. It is near rectangular and positioned on a promontory between valleys (SO 127155). The north and south sides are protected by the edges of the promontory. The east and west sides have a bank and ditch defence. The east bank measures about 16 feet wide and 2 feet high. The ditch is only visible as crop marks. The entrances may have been at the place where there is a gap near the centre of the east bank, and also at a hollow-way in the south scarp (RCHME, 1976, 87–89). When I visited the area of this fort, I was unable to clearly identify any earthworks that I could confirm as being a part of the original fort structure.

Nottingham Hill (Gotherington)

This is a large bi-vallate hill-fort, enclosing an area of 120 acres and positioned on a promontory of a spur escarpment (SO 987282) nearby to Cleeve Cloud. On the south-east side crossing the spur, there are two closely set banks, each with an outer ditch; the defences were 105 feet across overall. The other sides of this fort are defined by the scarp edges. The inner bank stands 5 feet above the interior, and 10 feet above the inner ditch. The outer bank is less large at 7 feet tall above the outer ditch. There is a hollow-way leading from lower ground into the ditch to the north (RCHME, 1976, 59).

A Bronze Age barrow cemetery and Bronze Age hoard have also been discovered at this multi-phase site (Copeland, 2013, 53–54). On visiting the area near where the fort is located, I was not able to identify any remains due to the inaccessibility of this site.

Owlpen (Nympsfield)

At this site there is a supposed multivallate hill-fort that once existed (SO 800000); however this is not confirmed. There are some remains of a substantial bank with evidence of slight ditches on either side (RCHME, 1976, 91). The positioning of this fort is on sloping ground, but does not have high ground advantage. I was able to see this site in the distance from a nearby road.

Pinbury Hillfort (Duntisbourne Rouse)

Pinbury Hillfort: the area where this fort was previously inhabited.

A univallate defended fort, positioned on a spur in between valleys (SO 958053), encloses an area of about 25 acres. There is a bank with an outer ditch to the north and east sides, which has been damaged by ploughing. There is another bank to the south-west that cuts across the tip of the spur. There is a scarp in between the banks at the south and the west. A 30-foot-wide gap in the east side bank is the entrance (RCHME, 1976, 48–49).

I was able to get close to this site via a footpath through a nearby field. Even though the remains were not clearly identifiable, it is clear that there is a raised height advantage as, although the ground level of close-by areas are of a similar height, the ground next to the fort is at a lower level on most sides.

Ring Hill (Haresfield)

This univallate defended hill-fort encloses an area of nearly 10 acres and is positioned on a spur of the Cotswold escarpment (SO 822090); positioned nearby is another fort, The Bulwarks. The defences consisted of a single bank without an external ditch, which surrounded the interior in a near-rectangular shape. The bank on the north and south sides measure from very slight up to 30 feet wide and 4 feet high. The bank to the east is about 2.5 feet high and follows the natural ridge above a gully. The west side at the tip of the spur has been damaged by quarrying (RCHME, 1976, 62–64).

Ring Hill: walking along the bank on a foggy day.

Ring Hill: the interior.

Ring Hill: the steep sides at this fort.

Ring Hill: some visible earthwork remains.

Ring Hill: the rampart defence curving around.

Ring Hill: the edge of this fort can be seen in the distance, to the right.

There are five gaps in the bank defences; two to the north are approached by terrace-ways. However, on the south side, two of these are partly as a result of quarrying. The other gap is approached by a hollow-way (RCHME, 1976, 62–64). The interior to this fort is now uneven, but the views of the surrounding areas are great.

When walking along the road between this fort and the Bulwarks, the short distance and visual presence of Ring Hill in the distance does suggest that perhaps these sites were connected.

Roel Camp (Sudeley)

This hill-fort is positioned on a ridge-top of Inferior Oolite (SP 047243), west of Roel Gate. It has a univallate defensive system. The bank measures some 20 feet across, and is 3 feet above the interior level and 6 feet above the outer ditch, which has been disturbed. The area enclosed is close to oval and covers 2.5 acres of a slightly domed area. There is a gap of 120 feet to the north, where perhaps the entrance was situated (RCHME, 1976, 112–113).

Roel Camp: a view of the interior area.

Roel Camp: some of the bank defences are slightly visible.

Roel Camp: the bank defence.

Roel Camp: Fort remains, with
good views into the distance.

I was able to get close to this site via a road that runs alongside the fort. From the
road I was able to identify the defences and get a view of this enclosure located on high
ground.

The Roundabout (Lyneham)

A univallate fort, near circular in shape and positioned on relatively level ground
(SP 299214). This enclosure covers an area of 4.5 acres and the bank and ditch
defences surround this area. The bank, 6 feet high in places, has a dry-stone wall
facing. Excavation has shown the U-shaped ditch to be 18 feet wide and 7 feet deep.
The original entrance perhaps is located to the north, where there is a gap in the bank
defence (Dyer, 1970, 53).

Seeing this site from the road, it is evident that the positioning is not the strongest
defensively; however, the defences do encompass the interior area.

The Roundabout: the earthwork remains, a site that has been quarried.

The Roundabout: the bank defences, seen from the road.

The Roundabout: the bank defences, seen within the trees.

Salmonsbury Camp (Bourton-On-The-Water)

An enclosure positioned between the Dikler and Windrush rivers at 425 feet above O.D. (SP 173208) and encloses a large area of 56 acres. The defences are bi-vallate, two banks each with an outer ditch. There is an annex of about 15 acres, where the banks and ditches extend south-east on an angle. Excavations took place during 1931–34, and the banks measure up to 3 feet high where they are best preserved. The inner bank is 60 feet across and its outer ditch was originally 36 feet wide and 12 feet deep. The outer bank, which has almost been levelled, measures 40 feet across; its V-shaped outer ditch is 18 feet wide and 9 feet deep (RCHME, 1976, 17–19).

The entrances were at the north-west and north-east, as well as a gap in the defences on the south-east side. An intermittent stream flows through the enclosed area and out towards the south-east, so there would have been a water supply for the inhabitants (RCHME, 1976, 17–19). On visiting this area, I was able to see the fort location in the distance from a nearby road but was unable to identify any earthwork remains clearly. Although the positioning of this fort was on low ground, this enclosure is still impressive, as it is large in size, with bi-vallate defences and a water source.

Shenberrow Hillfort (Stanton)

Positioned on a sloping spur of the Cotswold escarpment (SP 080334), an area of 2.5 acres is enclosed by bi-vallate defences. The entrance is positioned near the south-west corner, where there is a gap around 125 feet from the end of the bank.

Shenberrow Hillfort: the inner rampart.

The inner rampart is 30 feet wide and 5 feet high, while the inner ditch is 25 feet wide and 4 feet deep. The outer rampart is 25 feet wide and 2 feet high, while the ditch is 25 feet wide and 3 feet deep. There are parts of this site that have been levelled and are only visible as crop marks (RCHME, 1976, 109–110). However, there are remains of the defences visible today, while a pathway runs through the fort interior. This enclosure is D-shaped in plan (Darvill, 2011, 184).

There is another bank that runs parallel with the scarp edge, measuring 20 feet wide and 3 feet high – it has been damaged. There is evidence of an enclosed area within the interior of this fort outlined by banks. An excavation in 1935 showed that the inner rampart had a dry-stone revetment on its inner face and that the flat-bottomed ditch was 11 feet deep (RCHME, 1976, 109–110).

Although this hill-fort is small in area, its defences were comparatively of high stature, with two sets of defences protecting much of this site.

Shenberrow Hillfort: the interior area.

Shenberrow Hillfort: the rampart defences, seen from the outside.

Shenberrow Hillfort: a view of the approach from lower ground.

Shenberrow Hillfort: the high-ground advantage, seen from a lower position.

Shenberrow Hillfort: a view of distant areas, from the interior.

Sodbury Camp (Little Sodbury)

This fort has a bi-vallate defence system; it is near rectangular and encloses an area of 11 acres on the edge of a plateau (ST 760826) (RCHME, 1976, 103–104). This site, which is also known as a Roman Camp, was originally built during the Iron Age (Copeland, 2013, 136–138). The inner rampart is about 35 feet wide and 7 feet high above the interior level, and is lower along the scarp edge. The inner ditch is 30 feet wide and 7 feet deep, dropping around the north corner to follow a natural terrace for 400 feet and is 25 feet below the scarp edge. There is a low counterscarp bank that accompanies the ditch, from where it drops down to the terrace. There is a gap of about 50 feet between the inner ditch and the outer rampart. The outer rampart is 56 feet wide and up to 11 feet high with a berm measuring 12 feet wide; it was irregularly constructed and is apparently unfinished. The outer ditch is 45 feet wide and 6–10 feet deep on the east side, while at other points it is 3 feet or less (RCHME, 1976, 103–104).

The entrance positioned in the middle of the east side, where there is a gap in the bank and a corresponding causeway in the ditch. There is a second causeway in the ditch, 170 feet from the entrance to the north, which has a reduction in the size of the bank at this point. There are other features that were built within this site, including two parallel banks. A linear bank is built adjacent to the fort to the north, standing 1,000 feet. long, 45ft wide and between 2 feet and 6 inches high, with a 28-feet-wide ditch. This feature is possibly contemporary (RCHME, 1976, 103–104).

Sodbury Camp: the large rampart defence in the corner.

Sodbury Camp: the interior area.

Sodbury Camp: the outer bank defence on approach.

Sodbury Camp: this fort looks impressive from a distance.

The interior area covers a relatively large area and, situated on this flat ground, could have been used for a range of purposes, including farming or trade. This is an interesting position, as the lack of height advantage would have meant that any potential attackers would have been able to approach the site without using much physical exertion. However, the defences built at this site are very impressive and, when visiting this site, it is clear that these two lines of defence would have offered substantial protection to anyone trying to break through.

Sodbury Camp: the space in between the defences.

Sodbury Camp: in between the defences, next to the inner ditch.

Solsbury Hill (Batheaston)

This impressive univallate hill-fort, also known as Little Solsbury Hill, is positioned at the summit of the hill (ST 768679). On arrival at this site, the location is evidently a strong position, with the high, advantageous ground overlooking the surrounding areas.

Excavations in the mid-to-late 1950s have shown that this site was inhabited at different times, the first an occupied fort in the Iron Age. The rampart defences are dry-stone wall without a ditch as such and are not more than 3 feet tall; these were occupied with post-hole huts. After, perhaps, the collapse or destruction of the rampart, the second settlement occupation continued in *c.* 150 BC, from which time stone huts have been identified (OS Map 1961, Falconer & Adams, 1935, 183; Dowden, 1957, 18; Dowden, 1962, 177; AM England & Wales 1958, 67, cited in Pastscape, 1993).

Solsbury Hill: a view while walking along the edge.

Solsbury Hill: walking next to the defences.

Solsbury Hill: a great view of Bath.

Solsbury Hill: the steep sides to this fort.

Solsbury Hill: a view of the interior and defensive remains.

Solsbury Hill: looking along the rampart.

Walking around this fort with a spacious, enclosed interior area, the views that can be seen from this site are striking, especially those into the city of Bath. Some of the rampart remains are still visible today.

Stow Camp (Stow-On-The-Wold)

It is suggested that there was an Iron Age hill-fort located in this town (SP 195259) (Crawford, 1933, and Grundy, cited in Pastscape, 2000), the fort enclosing an area of 30 acres (RCHME, 1976, 111). It appears that this enclosure from the mid-first millennium BC took the place of an earlier site from the late second millennium BC (Parry 1999a, cited in Darvill, 2011, 186). On visiting this area, although the site was inaccessible, the positioning did seem a suitable site, overlooking certain nearby areas. Some possible earthworks are also slightly visible.

Trewsbury Fort (Coates)

This partly bi-vallate fort is positioned on a spur at the edge of a shallow valley (ST 981998) and encloses an area of about 12 acres. On the east and south sides, there are two widely separated banks, each with an outer ditch. The west and north sides have been damaged. The inner bank is 24 feet wide and 2.5 feet high, and has a 30-foot-wide and 3-foot-deep ditch. There is evidence of an exterior revetment wall, which was noted in 1966. The outer bank is 45 feet wide and 6 feet high, with the outer ditch measuring 35 feet wide and 4 feet deep. These outer defences join up with the inner defences in the south-west area. The entrance was in the north-east and has been damaged, with a second entrance in the outer defences. There is another gap, which perhaps is not original (RCHME, 1976, 32).

There is a pathway that runs alongside the location of this fort, but the site itself was inaccessible. The positioning of this fort is on relatively low ground in comparison to nearby areas, but there are substantial defences.

Uley Bury (Uley)

On a prominent spur of the Cotswold escarpment (ST 784989) is positioned this large and impressive hill-fort. The defences used at this site are univallate, and the fort is near rectangular in shape. The bank measures up to 35 feet wide and 4 feet high; the bank stands along the edges of a 30-foot- to 60-foot-wide terrace overall. The terrace was probably made by digging out the material to make the bank, and has a modern pathway around the fort. There is a scarp, which rises from the inner side of the terrace to the interior level, standing at 3 feet to 13 feet high. A scarp falls externally from the bank down an average of 30 feet to a narrow ledge, which has been disturbed. This apparently is not a ditch but was probably associated with the defences (RCHME, 1976, 121–122).

There are three entrances at this site: to the north, east and south. The entrance at the north corner has in-turned banks with a short hollow-way between them, accessible by a col. The east-corner entrance has overlapping bank ends associated with a hollow-way.

Uley Bury: walking along the edge.

Uley Bury: the rampart defence on the left, the interior area on the right.

Uley Bury: the steep sides to this fort.

Uley Bury: the sloping scarp to the interior.

At the entrance at the south corner there is another hollow-way, which is flanked by the extension of the bank on the west side and by two partly artificially built mounds at the edge of the terrace. This fort encloses 38 acres, 6 acres of which being the terrace; it is one of the largest forts in the Cotswolds (RCHME, 1976, 121–122).

From the approach, the top of the fort is noticeable from a distance and holds a commanding position in the landscape. This site would have relied greatly on its positioning to give visual impact (Darvill, 2011, 190). The steep climb to this site would have been an exhausting task before the built defences were even reached. It has a fantastic view of the surrounding areas and is a striking monument in this area. There is a relatively steep climb to reach the fort but, once at the summit, the ground is mostly level.

Uley Bury: the high positioning, overlooking the tops of trees.

Uley Bury: the steep approach.

Willersey Hill Camp (Willersey)

This hill-fort, which is positioned on the summit and north scarp of the hill (SP 117379), probably had bi-vallate defences. There are banks on the east and south-west sides, but no evidence that there was a bank on the north side. The two closely set banks, which had a ditch between them, measured 85 feet wide overall. The inner bank is 2 feet high above the interior and 8.5 feet above the ditch bottom. The outer bank stands 4 feet above the exterior ground, where there is no sign of an outer ditch. On the south side, there is an inner bank only; this is 6 feet tall and skirts the head of a narrow combe. It was recorded on a map by Isaac Taylor in 1777 as a sub-rectangular area covering some 40 acres (RCHME, 1976, 128–130). An excavation in 1987 uncovered a rock-cut ditch about 11 feet wide, forming part of an oval enclosure within the fort (Wills, 1988, cited in Darvill, 2011, 194).

After visiting this area, there is evidence of some of the bank remains at the golf course and close-by areas that are built on this site. However there has been much construction on this structure, which makes identifying original features difficult.

Windrush Camp (Windrush)

This univallate fort is positioned on ground (SP 181123) that slopes gently down from a ridge that is very slight and narrow, and is close to the fort on the east. This site is near circular in shape and encloses an area of just over 3 acres. The entrance is situated to the west, where there is a 25-foot gap in the bank. The bank is 25 feet wide and 5.5 feet above the outer ditch. The ditch is about 23 feet wide and it has generally been levelled, and so is difficult to identify (RCHME, 1976, 130).

This fort, which I accessed via a restricted byway, is positioned on near-level ground. It is accessible without any high-ground advantage to make the approach a challenge, The bank remains are clearly visible, however the defences do encompass all of the interior area and good views can be seen from a path that runs alongside the fort.

Windrush Camp: the bank defence.

Windrush Camp: the circular defences seen from the outside.

Windrush Camp: the defences stand out on approach.

Windrush Camp: the interior area, seen from the outside.

Summary

I hope that this book has equipped you with a basic understanding of hill-forts and demonstrated why they were and still are impressive structures in our landscape. Within the Cotswolds, there are some sites that are not accessible because, for example, they may be situated on privately owned land or are now not visible, as the earthworks have been worn away. However, there are many of forts that are accessible and that can be reached via Cotswold Way paths and other public footpaths.

The gate leading up to Uley Bury.

The pathway to Sodbury Camp.

I would encourage you to go and see some of these forts for yourself and build your own interpretation as to how and why they were built, what they were used for and what life would have been like for those who inhabited them. I would recommend these sites in particular to go and see:

Beckbury Camp
Brackenbury Ditches
Burhill
The Castles, Dowdeswell
Cleeve Cloud
Crickley Hill
Horton Camp
Kemerton Camp
Kimsbury Castle
Leckhampton Hill
Little Down
Ring Hill
Shenberrow Fort
Sodbury Camp
Solsbury Hill
Uley Bury

A view of Bath, seen on the way to Little Down.

Myself at Leckhampton Hill.

Bibliography

Copeland, T., *Archaeological Walking Guides: The Cotswold Way* (Gloucestershire: The History Press, 2013).

Cunliffe, B., *Iron Age Communities In Britain* (London: Routledge & Kegan Paul Ltd, 1974).

Darvill, T., *Prehistoric Gloucestershire* (Gloucestershire: Amberley Publishing, 2011).

Darvill, T., Stamper, P. and Timby, J., *Oxford Archaeological Guides: England* (Oxford: Oxford University Press, 2002).

Dyer, J., *Discovering Regional Archaeology: The Cotswolds and The Upper Thames* (Tring: Shire Publications, 1970).

Dyer, J., *Ancient Britain* (London: B. T. Batsford, 1990).

Forde-Johnston, J., *Hillforts of the Iron Age in England and Wales: A Survey of the Surface Evidence* (Liverpool: Liverpool University Press, 1976).

Guilbert, G., *Hill-Fort Studies: Essays For A. H. A. Hogg* (Leicester: Leicester University Press, 1981).

Harding, D.W., *Hillforts Later Prehistoric Earthworks in Britain and Ireland.* (London: Academic Press, 1976).

Hill, D. and Jesson, M., *The Iron Age and its Hill-Forts: Papers Presented to Sir Mortimer Wheeler* (Southampton: Southampton University Press, 1971).

Hogg, A. H. A., *Hill-Forts of Britain* (London: Hart-Davis, MacGibbon Ltd, 1975).

Macleod, J., *Batsford's Walking Guides: The Cotswolds* (London: Batsford, 2011).

Megaw, J. V. S., and Simpson, D. D. A., *Introduction to British Prehistory.* (Leicester: Leicester University Press, 1979).

Pastscape, 1968. HEWLETTS CAMP. [Online] Available at: http://www.pastscape .org.uk/hob.aspx?hob_id=117676&sort=4&search=all&criteria=hewletts camp&rational=q&recordsperpage=10 [accessed 08 April 2016].

Pastscape, 1993. SOLSBURY HILL. [Online] Available at: http://www.pastscape .org.uk/hob.aspx?hob_id=203323&sort=4&search=all&criteria=solsbury hill&rational=q&recordsperpage=10 [accessed 08 April 2016].

Pastscape, 1999. BURY WOOD CAMP. [Online] Available at: http://www.pastscape .org.uk/hob.aspx?hob_id=208476&sort=4&search=all&criteria=bury wood camp& rational=q&recordsperpage=10 [accessed 08 April 2016].

Pastscape, 2004. BATHAMPTON CAMP. [Online] Available at: http://www.pastscape. org.uk/hob.aspx?hob_id=203244&sort=4&search=all&criteria=bathampton camp&rational=q&recordsperpage=10 [accessed 08 April 2016].

Pastscape, 2004. MEON HILL. [Online] Available at: http://www.pastscape.org.uk /hob.aspx?hob_id=330738&sort=4&search=all&criteria=meon hill&rational=q& recordsperpage=10 [accessed 08 April 2016].

Pastscape, 2009. MONUMENT NO. 327538. [Online] Available at: http://www.pastscape. org.uk/hob.aspx?hob_id=327538&sort=4&search=all&criteria=dowdeswell& rational=q&recordsperpage=10&p=1&move=n&nor=46&recfc=0 [accessed 08 April 2016].

Pastscape, 2009. MONUMENT NO. 332307. [Online] Available at: http://www.pastscape. org.uk/hob.aspx?hob_id=332307&sort=4&search=all&criteria=idbury&rational= q&recordsperpage=10 [accessed 08 April 2016].

Pastscape, 2013. NADBURY CAMP. [Online] Available at: http://www.pastscape. org.uk/hob.aspx?hob_id=335146&sort=4&search=all&criteria=nadbury camp&rational=q&recordsperpage=10 [accessed 08 April 2016].

Pastscape, 2000. STOW CAMP. [Online] Available at: http://pastscape.org.uk/hob.aspx? hob_id=330170&sort=4&search=all&criteria=stow camp&rational=q&recordsper page=10 [accessed 24 April 2016].

Royal Commission on Historical Monuments (England), *Iron Age and Romano-British Monuments in the Gloucestershire Cotswolds* (London: Her Majesty's Stationary Office, 1976).